FRANCIS

SCRIPTURAE SACRAE AFFECTUS

Apostolic Letter on the Sixteen Hundredth Anniversary of the Death of Saint Jerome

Introduction by
Cardinal GIANFRANCO RAVASI

LIBRERIA
EDITRICE
VATICANA

© Copyright 2020 - Libreria Editrice Vaticana
00120 Città del Vaticano
Tel. 06.698.45780 - Fax 06.698.84716
E-mail: commerciale.lev@spc.va

ISBN 978-88-266-0510-4

www.vatican.va

www.libreriaeditricevaticana.com

INTRODUCTION

It was 30 September 420 in Bethlehem, near the cave of Christ's Nativity; Jerome the Dalmatian was closing his earthly existence, the plot line of which had been particularly varied and even tormented. Exactly 1600 years after that autumn day Pope Francis wished to dedicate an extensive and intense Apostolic Letter to him, which constitutes the substance of this small volume. The title, *Scripturae Sacrae Affectus*, derived from the Saint's memorial liturgy, represents an extraordinary synthesis of his personal experience and his works, indeed, almost an emblematic banner of one who is remembered by all as the translator par excellence of the Bible through the *Vulgate* which has spanned the centuries.

For this very reason his figure has been a capital point of reference for the history of western culture and even for art, and it is truly surprising that the Pope himself wished to evoke several "sapiential" artistic portraits, beginning from the "touching masterpiece" of the panel of the penitent Jerome in the wilderness that Leonardo da Vinci painted circa 1482 and which had a romantic storyline. Even the last hours lived by the Saint were represented by the majestic altarpiece in which Domenichino, between 1611 and 1614, focused on the extreme *Communion of St Jerome*, a work held, like the other, in the Vatican Pinacoteca. In a hieratic atmosphere the legendary "Lion of Bethlehem", by now debilitated, receives the Eucharist surrounded by his disciples and by the faithful Paula, witnesses of the monastic communities he founded.

* * *

The Apostolic Letter is a veritable historical-theological portrait of this passionate expert on the Word of God; it is a guide to follow his vast exegetic and spiritual work; it is an appeal to follow in his footsteps, "loving what he loved".

The clarity of the dictation and structure of the papal text is such that it requires no commentary, but only an attentive reading: each page is inlaid with highly suggestive citations derived from Jerome's writings. For this reason it is truly possible to almost hear his voice, with the range of tones, of accents, of the same sentiments of such a strong character and the typical features of biblical prophets with their vehemence and passion.

The complex sequence of biographical events distributed primarily between Rome and the Holy Land are reconstructed in a careful yet lively way, beginning with the famous Lenten turning point in 375 which we too wish to recall. Numbed by a fever, a sort of vision had opened in his mind. Standing before the divine Judge, "Asked who and what I was I replied: 'I am a Christian'. But He who presided said: 'You lie. You are a follower of Cicero and not of Christ'". This is how the Saint recounted the great turning point of his life in Letter 22 of the traditional catalogue, addressed to the faithful disciple Eustochium.

In another letter, he wrote: "I betook myself to a brother who before his conversion had been a Jew and asked him to teach me Hebrew. Thus, after having familiarised myself with the pointedness of Quintilian, the fluency of Cicero, the seriousness of Fronto and the gentleness of Pliny, I began to learn my letters anew and to study to pronounce words both harsh and guttural. What labour I spent upon this task, what difficulties I went through, how often I despaired, how often I gave over and then in my eagerness to learn commenced again, can be attested both by myself the subject of this misery and by those who then lived with me". Thus began the great adventure that became renowned with the name *Vulgate*, the development of a "popular" Latin translation of the Bible.

The Pope follows from that moment the entire itinerary, through certain fascinating and moving verses, of the Christian experience of Jerome, whose heart lies in love for Sacred Scripture which he faces in its twofold dimension of "letter" and "spirit". The fundamental axis of his human and spiritual journey lies in his work as a translator, indeed embodied in the *Vulgate*, "the sweetest fruit of the arduous sowing" of his literary and historical-critical studies. Pope Francis offers in this regard not only a series of valuable annotations on the significance of this work in its basic characteristics, but also on the ecclesial importance it records. Above all it captures the highly original soul that is also at the root of every qualified translation that continues even today to be revealed through the endless versions of the Bible in the most diverse languages.

To translate, in fact, is an act of inculturation and, to this point, explicitly recovering a meaningful reflection developed from contemporary thought (P. Ricoeur, L. Wittgenstein, G. Steiner), the Pope establishes "an analogy between translation as an act of 'linguistic' hospitality and other forms of hospitality. This is why translation does not concern language alone but really reflects a broader ethical decision connected with an entire approach to life. Without translation, different linguistic communities would be unable to communicate among themselves; we would close the doors of history to one another and negate the possibility of building a culture of encounter. In effect, without translation there can be no such hospitality; indeed hostility would increase. A translator is a bridge builder. How many hasty judgments are made, how many condemnations and conflicts arise from the fact that we do not understand the language of other persons and fail to apply ourselves, with firm hope, to the endless demonstration of love that translation represents".

* * *

With all the critical reservations, often understandable considering the different chronological and cultural coordinates and our different philological sensitivity, the *Vulgate* constituted not only a literary monument to late Latin, but it shaped the theological language of Western Christians. In truth success came to Jerome's work only a couple of centuries later. It was Saint Gregory the

Great, Pope from 590 to 605, who used Jerome's translation for his exegetic and spiritual writings, followed by his near contemporary Isidore of Seville and the Venerable Bede, who died in 735. The river of copies grew drastically, dragging with it all kinds of debris, that is, scribal errors, intentional mutations, marginal variations, contamination with other ancient Latin versions. Then revision and codification work was required, giving rise to veritable textual typologies represented by families of codes, conventionally grouped according to geographical areas.

Thus was born the so-called "Italian" model, named from the *Vulgate*'s primary sphere of dissemination: it must not be forgotten that the sixth century historian and theologian Cassiodorus, along with Saint Gregory, crafted the adoption of Jerome's version for reading and studying the Bible within his *Vivarium*, the "university" he founded in his lands of Squillace in Calabria. There was a "Gaelic" typology linked to Alcuin, entrusted with this work by Charles the Great (8th-9th centuries); other models appeared in Spain and Ireland. It is not necessary for our purposes to outline the profile of this branched delta where the river of the *Vulgate* landed, nor to describe the revisions made by various people, such as for example Saint Peter Damian and Lanfranco di Pavia in the 11th century. The most widespread text that followed its path in the centuries that followed until the Renaissance was the so-called *Biblia Parisiensis*, in use at the University of Paris, however one of the least perfect forms in the long life of the *Vulgate*.

It was only in the Council of Trent that, after the authenticity of the *Vulgate* was affirmed as the official biblical text of the Catholic Church (8 April 1546) – on whose specific value the Apostolic Letter offers an essential and precise indication – that the vote for a more rigorous "typical edition" was expressed.

The guidance of the Council Fathers was fulfilled only on 9 November 1592, after difficult events that involved five Popes (Pius IV, Pius V, Sixtus V, Gregory XIV, Clement VIII). The definitive edition was then published with the title *Biblia Sacra Vulgatae editionis Sixti Quinti Pont. iussu recognita atque edita*. In the 1604 Lyons edition the name of Clement VIII was also added, and henceforth the "Sixtus-Clementine Bible" was spoken of. In subsequent centuries revisions were constant until the proposed detail of the *Nova Vulgata* promulgated by Saint John Paul II in 1979 and explicitly cited in the Letter.

It is a fact that, even with the differences of eras, the *Vulgate* still exerts an undoubted literary fascination today, also for its use in the history of art and music. Moreover, as stated, in some way it has conditioned theological thought and vocabulary. Now, French scholar Georges Mounin has ironically defined every good translation as a *belle infidèle*, beautiful yes, but with a degree of infidelity with respect to the original matrix, above all when involving different linguistic and cultural systems. He proceeded in the wake of the great Cervantes, the author of *Don Quixote*, convinced that every version was like the dull back side of a fine tapestry. The problems raised by translating a text are not, in fact, only linguistic-literary but hermeneutic, especially when there is a "sacred" Scripture involved. However, still today Jerome remains, precisely in this sense, an emblem of merit and method, with his rigour and his freedom, with his knowledge and his creativity.

* * *

But going beyond strictly critical questions the Pope, almost underlying the whole text, guides the ecclesial community in this centenary celebration to understand the substantial legacy of Saint Jerome, that is, the love created from the study of and vital coherence to the Word of God. This is a theme constantly exalted by the ecclesial Magisterium, particularly the statements of the Second

Vatican Council with *Dei Verbum*, the Apostolic Exhortation *Verbum Domini* which Benedict XVI issued precisely in memory of the Saint on 30 September 2010, *Evangelii Gaudium* and *Aperuit Illis* by Pope Francis himself, nor can we forget that in the parallel 15th centenary of Jerome's death, in 1920 Benedict XV promulgated the Encyclical *Spiritus Paraclitus*. Indeed, "the distinctive feature of Saint Jerome's spirituality was undoubtedly his passionate love for the Word of God entrusted to the Church in sacred Scripture".

Other features emerge from the pages of the Apostolic Letter. In particular his theoretical and practical commitment to monastic life, as well as his profound love for the Virgin Mother who "pondered in her heart" (*Lk* 2:19, 51) "because she was a holy woman, had read the sacred Scriptures, knew the prophets, and recalled that the angel Gabriel had said to her the same things that the prophets had foretold".

One feature, usually less emphasized but which Pope Francis instead develops, is the Saint's connection with the Chair of Peter. Also prevailing in the Father of the Church is that christological axis that guides not only his faith but also his exegesis. In fact, what he himself wrote about his friend Nepotian also applies to him: "by constant reading and long-continued meditation he had made his breast a library of Christ".

This preface – dedicated to a truly luminous text as are these pages consecrated by Pope Francis to a Father of the Church of an ardent and even provocative temperament, but also of clear and warm faith as Saint Jerome was – could easily have a seal in the same pontifical document. The final summary, in fact, is to be sought in the Letter's concluding appeal. Returning to the image just offered of the "library of Christ", the Pope reminds us that Jerome's is a living library that "continues to teach us the meaning of Christ's love, a love that is inseparable from an encounter with his word. This is why the present anniversary can be seen as a summons to love what Jerome loved, to rediscover his writings and to let ourselves be touched by his robust spirituality, which can be described in essence as a restless and impassioned desire for a greater knowledge of the God who chose to reveal himself. How can we not heed, in our day, the advice that Jerome unceasingly gave to his contemporaries: 'Read the divine Scriptures constantly; never let the sacred volume fall from your hand'?".

Cardinal GIANFRANCO RAVASI

FRANCIS

Apostolic Letter

Scripturae Sacrae Affectus

on the Sixteen Hundredth Anniversary
of the Death of Saint Jerome

Devotion to sacred Scripture, a "living and tender love" for the written word of God: this is the legacy that Saint Jerome bequeathed to the Church by his life and labours. Now, on the sixteen hundredth anniversary of his death, those words taken from the opening prayer of his liturgical Memorial[1] give us an essential insight into this outstanding figure in the Church's history and his immense love for Christ. That "living and tender love" flowed, like a great river feeding countless streams, into his tireless activity as a scholar, translator and exegete. Jerome's profound knowledge of the Scriptures, his zeal for making their teaching known, his skill as an interpreter of texts, his ardent and at times im-

[1] *"Deus qui beato Hieronymo presbitero suavem et vivum Scripturae Sacrae affectum tribuisti, da, ut populus tuus verbo tuo uberius alatur et in eo fontem vitae inveniet"*. Collecta Missae Sanctae Hieronymi, *Missale Romanum*, editio typica tertia, Civitas Vaticana, 2002.

petuous defence of Christian truth, his asceticism and harsh eremitical discipline, his expertise as a generous and sensitive spiritual guide – all these make him, sixteen centuries after his death, a figure of enduring relevance for us, the Christians of the twenty-first century.

Introduction

On 30 September 420, Saint Jerome died in Bethlehem, in the community that he had founded near the grotto of the Nativity. He thus entrusted himself to the Lord whom he had always sought and known in the Scriptures, the same Lord whom, as a Judge, he had already encountered in a feverish dream, possibly during the Lenten season of 375. That dream proved to be a decisive turning point in his life, an occasion of conversion and change in outlook. He saw himself dragged before the Judge. As he himself recalled: "Questioned about my state, I responded that I was a Christian. But the Judge retorted: 'You lie! You are a Ciceronian, not a Christian'".[2] Jerome had loved from his youth the limpid beauty of the Latin classics, whereas the writings of the Bible had initially struck him

---

[2] *Epistula* (hereafter *Ep.*) 22, 30: CSEL 54, 190.

as uncouth and ungrammatical, too harsh for his refined literary taste.

That experience inspired Jerome to devote himself entirely to Christ and his word, and to strive through his translations and commentaries to make the divine writings increasingly accessible to others. It gave his life a new and more decisive orientation: he was to become a servant of the word of God, in love, as it were, with the "flesh of Scripture". Thus, in the pursuit of knowledge that marked his entire life, he put to good use his youthful studies and Roman education, redirecting his scholarship to the greater service of God and the ecclesial community.

As a result, Saint Jerome became one of the great figures of the ancient Church in the period known as the golden age of patristics. He served as a bridge between East and West. A youthful friend of Rufinus of Aquileia, he knew Ambrose and was frequently in correspondence with Augustine. In the East, he knew Gregory of Nazianzus, Didymus the Blind and Epiphanius of Salamis. The Christian iconographic tradition presents him, in the company of Augustine, Ambrose and Gregory the Great, as one of the four great Doctors of the Western Church.

My predecessors have honoured Saint Jerome on various occasions. A century ago, on the fifteenth centenary of his death, Benedict XV dedicated his Encyclical Letter *Spiritus Paraclitus* (15 September 1920) to Jerome, presenting him to the world as *"doctor maximus explanandis Scripturis"*.[3] More recently, Benedict XVI devoted two successive catecheses to his person and works.[4] Now on the 1600th anniversary of his death, I too desire to commemorate Saint Jerome and to emphasize once more the timeliness of his message and teachings, beginning with his immense love for the Scriptures.

Indeed, as a sure guide and authoritative witness, Jerome in some sense dominated both the XII Assembly of the Synod of Bishops devoted to the Word of God,[5] and the Apostolic Exhortation *Verbum Domini* of my predecessor Benedict XVI, published on the feast day of the Saint, 30 September 2010.[6]

---

[3] *AAS* 12 (1920), 385-423.

[4] Cf. General Audiences of 7 and 14 November 2007: *Insegnamenti*, III, 2 (2007), 553-556; 586-591.

[5] SYNOD OF BISHOPS, Twelfth Ordinary General Assembly, *Message to the People of God* (24 October 2008).

[6] Cf. *AAS* 102 (2010), 681-787.

The journey of Saint Jerome's life traversed the roads of the Roman Empire between Europe and the East. Born around 345 in Stridon, on the border between Dalmatia and Pannonia, in present-day Croatia and Slovenia, he received a solid upbringing in a Christian family. As was the custom in those times, he was baptized as an adult sometime between 358 and 364, while studying rhetoric in Rome. During his Roman sojourn, he became an insatiable reader of the Latin classics, studying under the most celebrated teachers of rhetoric then living.

Following his studies, he undertook a long journey through Gaul, which brought him to the imperial city of Trier, now in Germany. There he first encountered Eastern monasticism as disseminated by Saint Athanasius. The result was a deep and enduring desire for that experience, which led him to Aquileia, where, with a few of his friends, "a choir of the blessed",[7] he inaugurated a period of life in common.

Around the year 374, passing through Antioch, he decided to retire to the desert of Chal-

---

[7] *Chronicum* 374: PL 27, 697-698.

cis, in order to realize in an ever more radical manner an ascetical life in which great space was reserved for the study of the biblical languages, first Greek and then Hebrew. He studied under a Christianized Jew who introduced him to the knowledge of Hebrew and its sounds, which he found "harsh and aspirate".[8]

Jerome consciously chose the desert and the eremitic life for their deeper meaning as a locus of fundamental existential decisions, of closeness and encounter with God. There, through contemplation, interior trials and spiritual combat, he came to understand more fully his own weakness, his own limits and those of others. There too, he discovered the importance of tears.[9] The desert taught him sensitivity to God's presence, our necessary dependence on him and the consolations born of his mercy. Here, I am reminded of an apocryphal story in which Jerome asks the Lord: "What do you want of me?" To which Christ replies: "You have not yet given me everything". "But Lord, I have given you all sorts of things". "One thing you have not given

[8] *Ep.* 125, 12: CSEL 56, 131.
[9] Cf. *Ep.* 122, 3: CSEL 56, 63.

me". "What is that?" "Give me your sins, so that I may rejoice in forgiving them once more".[10]

We then find him in Antioch, where he was ordained a priest by the bishop of that city, Paulinus, and later, about 379, in Constantinople, where he met Gregory of Nazianzus and continued his studies. He translated from Greek into Latin several important works (the homilies of Origen and the Chronicle of Eusebius) and was present for the Council celebrated there in 381. Those years of study revealed his generous enthusiasm and a blessed thirst for knowledge that made him tireless and passionate in his work. As he put it: "From time to time I despaired; often I gave up, but then I went back out of a stubborn will to learn". The "bitter seed" of his studies was to produce "savoury fruits".[11]

In 382, Jerome returned to Rome and placed himself at the service of Pope Damasus who, appreciating his outstanding gifts, made him one of his close associates. There Jerome engaged in a constant activity, without however neglecting spiritual matters. On the Aventine, supported

[10] Cf. *Morning Meditation*, 10 December 2015. The anecdote is related in A. LOUF, *Sotto la guida dello Spirito*, Qiqaion, Mangano (BI), 1990, 154-155.

[11] Cf. *Ep.* 125, 12: CSEL 56, 131.

by aristocratic Roman women intent on a radically evangelical life, like Marcella, Paula and her daughter Eustochium, he created a cenacle devoted to the reading and the rigorous study of Scripture. Jerome acted as exegete, teacher and spiritual guide. At this time, he undertook a revision of the earlier Latin translations of the Gospels and perhaps other parts of the New Testament as well. He continued his work of translating Origen's homilies and biblical commentaries, engaged in a flurry of letter writing, publically refuted heretical writers, at times intemperately but always moved by the sincere desire to defend the true faith and the deposit of Scripture.

This intense and productive period was interrupted by the death of Pope Damasus. Jerome found himself forced to leave Rome and, followed by friends and some women desirous of continuing the experience of spiritual life and biblical study already begun, left for Egypt, where he met the great theologian Didymus the Blind. He then travelled to Palestine and in 386 settled definitively in Bethlehem. He resumed his study of the biblical texts, texts now anchored in the very places of which they spoke.

The importance he attributed to the holy places is seen not only by his decision to live in Palestine from 386 until his death, but also by the assistance he gave to pilgrims. In Bethlehem, a place close to his heart, he founded in the environs of the grotto of the Nativity, "twin" monasteries, male and female, with hospices to provide lodging for pilgrims to the holy places. This was yet another sign of his generosity, for he made it possible for many others to see and touch the places of salvation history, and to find both cultural and spiritual enrichment.[12]

In his attentive listening to the Scriptures, Jerome came to know himself and to find the face of God and of his brothers and sisters. He was also confirmed in his attraction to community life. His desire to live with friends, as he had in Aquileia, led him to establish monastic communities in order to pursue the cenobitic ideal of religious life. There, the monastery is seen as a "palaestra" for training men and women "who consider themselves least of all, in order to be first among all", content with poverty and capable of teaching others by their own style of life. Jerome considered it a formative experience to live "under the governance of a single superior and in the company of

<hr>

[12] Cf. Apostolic Exhortation *Verbum Domini*, 89: *AAS* 102 (2010), 761-762.

many" in order to learn humility, patience, silence and meekness, in the awareness that "the truth does not love dark corners and does not seek grumblers".[13] He also confessed that he "yearned for the close cells of the monastery" and "desired the eagerness of ants, where all work together, nothing belongs to any individual, and everything belongs to everyone".[14]

Jerome saw his studies not as a pleasant pastime and an end unto itself, but rather as a spiritual exercise and a means of drawing closer to God. His classical training was now directed to the deeper service of the ecclesial community. We think of the assistance he gave to Pope Damasus and his commitment to the instruction of women, especially in the study of Hebrew, from the time of the first cenacle on the Aventine. In this way, he enabled Paula and Eustochium to "enter the serried ranks of translators",[15] and, something unheard of in those days, to read and chant the Psalms in the original language.[16]

---

[13] Cf. *Ep.* 125, 9.15.19: CSEL 56, 128.133-134.139.
[14] *Vita Malchi monachi captivi*, 7, 3: PL 23, 59-60.
[15] *Praefatio in Librum Esther*, 2: PL 28, 1505.
[16] Cf. *Ep.* 108, 26: CSEL 55, 344-345.

His great erudition was employed in offering a necessary service to those called to preach the Gospel. As he reminded his friend Nepotianus: "the word of the priest must be flavoured by the reading of Scripture. I do not wish that you be a disclaimer or charlatan of many words, but one who understands the sacred doctrine (*mysterii*) and knows deeply the teachings (*sacramentorum*) of your God. It is typical of the ignorant to play around with words and to garner the admiration of inexpert people by speaking quickly. Those who are shameless often explain that which they do not know and pretend to be a great expert only because they succeed in persuading others".[17]

Jerome's years in Bethlehem, to the time of his death in 420, were the most fruitful and intense period of his life, completely dedicated to the study of Scripture and to the monumental work of translating the entire Old Testament on the basis of the original Hebrew. At the same time, he commented on the prophetic books, the Psalms and the letters of Paul, and wrote guides to the study of the Bible. The deep learning that flowed over into his works was the fruit of a collaborative effort, from the copying and

---

[17] *Ep.* 52, 8: CSEL 54, 428-429; cf. *Verbum Domini*, 60: *AAS* 102 (2010), 739.

collating of manuscripts to further reflection and discussion. As he put it: "I have never ever trusted in my own powers to study the divine volumes… I have the habit of asking questions, also about that which I thought I knew and even more so about that of which I was not sure".[18] Conscious of his limitations, he asked for constant prayer and intercession for his efforts to translate the sacred texts "in the same Spirit by whom they were written".[19] Nor did he fail to translate works by authors indispensable for exegesis, such as Origen, "in order to make them available to those who would like to study this material more deeply and systematically".[20]

As an enterprise carried out within the community and at the service of the community, Jerome's scholarly activity can serve as an example of synodality for us and for our own time. It can also serve as a model for the Church's various cultural institutions, called to be "places where knowledge becomes service, for no genuine and integral human development can occur without a body of knowledge that is the fruit of coop-

[18] *Praefatio in Librum Paralipomenon LXX*, 1.10-15: *Sources Chrétiennes* 592, 340.

[19] *Praefatio in Pentateuchum*: PL 28, 184.

[20] *Ep.* 80, 3: CSEL 55, 105.

eration and leads to greater cooperation".[21] The basis of such communion is Scripture, which we cannot read merely on our own: "The Bible was written by the People of God for the People of God, under the inspiration of the Holy Spirit. Only in this communion with the People of God can we truly enter as a 'we' into the heart of the truth that God himself wishes to convey to us".[22]

His solid experience of a life nurtured by the word of God enabled Jerome, through the many letters he wrote, to become a spiritual guide. He became a fellow traveller to many, for he was convinced that "no skill can be learned without a teacher". Thus he wrote to Rusticus: "This is what I would like to make you understand, taking you by the hand like an ancient mariner, the survivor of several shipwrecks, attempting to teach a young sailor".[23] From his peaceful corner of the world, he followed the course of human affairs in an age of great upheaval, marked by events like the sack of Rome in 410, which affected him deeply.

---

[21] *Message on the Occasion of the Twenty-fourth Public Session of the Pontifical Academies*, 4 December 2019: *L'Osservatore Romano*, 6 December 2019, p. 8.

[22] *Verbum Domini*, 30: *AAS* 102 (2010), 709.

[23] *Ep.* 125, 15.2: CSEL 56, 133.120.

In those letters he dealt with doctrinal controversies, constantly in defence of sound doctrine. His letters also show the value he placed on relationships. Jerome could be forceful but also gentle, sincerely concerned for others, and, since "love is priceless",[24] enthusiastic in showing genuine affection. This can also be seen from the fact that he offered his works of translation and commentary as a *munus amicitiae*. They were to be a gift above all for his friends, correspondents and those to whom his works were dedicated – all of whom he begged to read them with a friendly rather than a critical eye – but also for his readers, his contemporaries and those who would come after them.[25]

Jerome spent the last years of his life in the prayerful reading of Scripture, both privately and in community, in contemplation and in serving his brothers and sisters through his writings. All this in Bethlehem, near the grotto where the eternal Word was born of the Virgin Mary. For he was convinced that "they are blessed who bear within them the cross, the resurrection, the places of Christ's nativity and ascension! Blessed

---

[24] *Ep.* 3, 6: CSEL 54, 18.
[25] Cf. *Praefatio in Librum Iosue*, 1, 9-12: SCh 592, 316.

are they who have Bethlehem in their heart, in whose heart Christ is born each day!".[26]

The "sapiential" aspect of Jerome's life

To understand Saint Jerome's personality fully, we need to unite two dimensions that characterized his life as a believer: on the one hand, an absolute and austere consecration to God, renouncing all human satisfaction for love of Christ crucified (cf. *1 Cor* 2:2; *Phil* 3:8.10), and on the other, a commitment to diligent study, aimed purely at an ever deeper understanding of the Christian mystery. This double witness, wondrously offered by Saint Jerome, can serve as a model above all for monks, since all who live a life of asceticism and prayer are urged to devote themselves to the exacting labour of research and reflection. It is likewise a model for scholars, who should always keep in mind that knowledge has religious value only if it is grounded in an exclusive love for God, apart from all human ambition and worldly aspiration.

These two aspects of his life have found expression in the history of art. Saint Jerome was frequently depicted by great masters of Western

---

[26] *Homilia in Psalmum 95*: PL 26, 1181.

painting following two distinct iconographic traditions. One can be described as primarily monastic and penitential, showing Jerome with a body emaciated by fasting, living in the desert, kneeling or prostrate on the ground, in many cases clutching a rock and beating his breast, his eyes turned towards the crucified Lord. In this line, we find the moving masterpiece of Leonardo da Vinci now in the Vatican Museums. Another tradition shows Jerome in the garb of a scholar, seated at his writing desk, intent on translating and commenting on the sacred Scriptures, surrounded by scrolls and parchments, devoted to defending the faith through his erudition and his writings. Albrecht Dürer, to cite one famous example, portrayed him more than once in this pose.

The two aspects are brought together in the painting by Caravaggio located in the Borghese Gallery in Rome: indeed in a single scene the elderly ascetic is shown dressed simply in a red robe with a skull on his table, a symbol of the vanity of earthly realities; but at the same time he is evidently depicted as a scholar, his eyes fixed on a book as his hand dips a quill into an inkwell – the typical act of a writer.

These two "sapiential" aspects were very much evident in Jerome's own life. If, as a true "Lion of Bethlehem", he could be violent in his language, it was always in the service of a truth to which he was unconditionally committed. As he explained in the first of his writings, the *Life of Saint Paul, Hermit of Thebes*, lions can roar but also weep.[27] What might at first appear as two separate aspects of Saint Jerome's character were joined by the Holy Spirit through a process of interior maturation.

Love for sacred Scripture

The distinctive feature of Saint Jerome's spirituality was undoubtedly his passionate love for the word of God entrusted to the Church in sacred Scripture. All the Doctors of the Church – particularly those of the early Christian era – drew the content of their teaching explicitly from the Bible. Yet Jerome did so in a more systematic and distinctive way.

Exegetes in recent times have come to appreciate the narrative and poetic genius of the Bible and its great expressive quality. Jerome instead emphasized in sacred Scripture the hum-

[27] Cf. *Vita S. Pauli primi eremitae*, 16, 2: PL 23, 28.

ble character of God's revelation, set down in the rough and almost primitive cadences of the Hebrew language in comparison to the refinement of Ciceronian Latin. He devoted himself to the study of sacred Scripture not for aesthetic reasons, but – as is well known – only because Scripture had led him to know Christ. Indeed, ignorance of Scripture is ignorance of Christ.[28]

Jerome teaches us that not only should the Gospels and the apostolic Tradition present in the Acts of the Apostles and in the Letters be studied and commented on, but that the entire Old Testament is indispensable for understanding the truth and the riches of Christ.[29] The Gospel itself gives evidence of this: it speaks to us of Jesus as the Teacher who appeals to Moses, the Prophets and the Psalms (cf. *Lk* 4:16-21; 24:27.44-47) in order to explain his own mystery. The preaching of Peter and Paul in the Acts of the Apostles is likewise rooted in the Old Testament, apart from which we cannot fully understand the figure of the Son of God, the Messiah and Saviour. Nor should the Old Testament be thought of merely as a vast rep-

[28] Cf. *In Isaiam Prologus:* PL 24, 17.
[29] Cf. SECOND VATICAN ECUMENICAL COUNCIL, Dogmatic Constitution on Divine Revelation *Dei Verbum*, 14.

ertoire of citations that prove the fulfilment of the ancient prophecies in the person of Jesus of Nazareth. Rather, only in light of the Old Testament prefigurements is it possible to know more profoundly the meaning of the Christ event as revealed in his death and resurrection. Today we need to rediscover, in catechesis and preaching, as well as in theological exposition, the indispensable contribution of the Old Testament, which should be read and digested as a priceless source of spiritual nourishment (cf. *Ez* 3:1-11; *Rev* 10:8-11).[30]

Jerome's complete devotion to Scripture is shown by his impassioned way of speaking and writing, similar to that of the ancient prophets. From them, this Doctor of the Church drew the inner fire that became a vehement and explosive word (cf. *Jer* 5:14; 20:9; 23:29; *Mal* 3:2; *Sir* 48:1; *Mt* 3:11; *Lk* 12:49) necessary for expressing the burning zeal of one who serves the cause of God. As with Elijah, John the Baptist and the Apostle Paul, indignation at lies, hypocrisy and false teaching inflamed Jerome's speech, making it provocative and seemingly harsh. We can better understand

[30] Cf. ibid.

the polemical dimension of his writings if we read them in the light of the most authentic prophetic tradition. Jerome thus emerges as a model of uncompromising witness to the truth that employs the harshness of reproof in order to foster conversion. By the intensity of his expressions and images, he shows the courage of a servant desirous not of pleasing others, but his Lord alone (*Gal* 1:10), for whose sake he expended all his spiritual energy.

The study of sacred Scripture

Saint Jerome's impassioned love for the divine Scriptures was steeped in obedience. First, to God who revealed himself in words that demand a reverent hearing,[31] and, then to those in the Church who represent the living Tradition that interprets the revealed message. The "obedience of faith" (*Rom* 1:5; 16:26) is not, however, a mere passive reception of something already known; on the contrary it demands an active personal effort to understand what was spoken. We can think of Saint Jerome as a "servant" of the word, faithful and industrious, entirely devoted to fostering

---

[31] Cf. ibid., 7.

in his brothers and sisters in faith a more adequate understanding of the sacred "deposit" entrusted to them (cf. *1 Tim* 6:20; *2 Tim* 1:14). Without an understanding of what was written by the inspired authors, the word of God itself is deprived of its efficacy (cf. *Mt* 13:19) and love for God cannot spring up.

Biblical passages are not always immediately accessible. As Isaiah said (29:11), even for those who know how to "read" – that is, those who have had a sufficient intellectual training – the sacred book appears "sealed", hermetically closed to interpretation. A witness is needed to intervene and provide the key to its liberating message, which is Christ the Lord. He alone is able to break the seal and open the book (cf. *Rev* 5:1-10) and in this way unveil its wondrous outpouring of grace (*Lk* 4:17-21). Many, even among practising Christians, say openly that they are not able to read it (cf. *Is* 29:12), not because of illiteracy, but because they are unprepared for the biblical language, its modes of expression and its ancient cultural traditions. As a result the biblical text becomes indecipherable, as if it were written in an unknown alphabet and an esoteric tongue.

This shows the need for the mediation of an interpreter, who can exercise a "diaconal" function on behalf of the person who cannot understand the meaning of the prophetic message. Here we think of the deacon Philip, sent by the Lord to approach the chariot of the eunuch who was reading a passage from Isaiah (53:7-8), without being able to unlock its meaning. "Do you understand what you are reading?" asked Philip, and the eunuch replied: "How can I, unless someone guides me?" (*Acts* 8:30-31).[32]

Jerome can serve as our guide because, like Philip (cf. *Acts* 8:35), he leads every reader to the mystery of Jesus, while responsibly and systematically providing the exegetical and cultural information needed for a correct and fruitful reading of the Scriptures.[33] In an integrated and skilful way he employed all the methodological resources available in his day – competence in the languages in which the word of God was handed down, careful analysis and examination of manuscripts, detailed archeological research, as well as knowledge of the history of interpretation – in order to point to a correct understanding of the inspired Scriptures.

[32] Cf. SAINT JEROME, *Ep.* 53, 5: CSEL 54, 451.
[33] Cf. SECOND VATICAN ECUMENICAL COUNCIL, Dogmatic Constitution on Divine Revelation *Dei Verbum*, 12.

This outstanding aspect of the activity of Saint Jerome is also of great importance for the Church in our own time. If, as *Dei Verbum* teaches, the Bible constitutes as it were "the soul of sacred theology"[34] and the spiritual support of the Christian life,[35] the interpretation of the Bible must necessarily be accompanied by specific skills.

Centres of excellence for biblical research – such as the Pontifical Biblical Institute in Rome, and the École Biblique and the Studium Biblicum Franciscanum in Jerusalem – and for patristic research, like the Augustinianum in Rome, certainly serve this purpose, but every Faculty of Theology should strive to ensure that the teaching of sacred Scripture is carried out in such a way that students are provided with necessary training in interpretative skills, both in the exegesis of texts and in biblical theology as a whole. Sadly, the richness of Scripture is neglected or minimized by many because they were not afforded a solid grounding in this area. Together with a greater emphasis on the study of Scripture in ecclesiastical programmes of training for priests and catechists, efforts should also be made to provide all the faithful with the

[34] Ibid., 24.
[35] Cf. ibid., 25.

resources needed to be able to open the sacred book and draw from it priceless fruits of wisdom, hope and life.[36]

Here I would recall an observation made by Pope Benedict XVI in the Apostolic Exhortation *Verbum Domini*: "The [sacramental nature] of the word can be understood by analogy with the real presence of Christ under the appearances of the consecrated bread and wine… Saint Jerome speaks of the way we ought to approach both the Eucharist and the word of God: 'We are reading the sacred Scriptures. For me, the Gospel is the body of Christ; for me, the holy Scriptures are his teaching. And when he says: *whoever does not eat my flesh and drink my blood* (*Jn* 6:53), even though these words can also be understood of the [Eucharistic] Mystery, Christ's body and blood are really the word of Scripture, God's teaching'".[37]

Sadly, many Christian families seem unable – as was prescribed in the Torah (cf. *Dt* 6:6) – to introduce their children to the word of the Lord in all its beauty and spiritual power. This led me to institute the Sunday of the Word of God[38] as

---

[36] Cf. ibid., 21.

[37] N. 56; cf. *In Psalmum 147*: CCL 78, 337-338.

[38] Cf. Apostolic Letter Motu Proprio *Aperuit Illis*, 30 September 2019.

38

a means of encouraging the prayerful reading of
the Bible and greater familiarity with God's word.[39]
All other expressions of piety will thus be enriched
with meaning, placed in their proper perspective
and directed to the fulfilment of faith in complete
adherence to the mystery of Christ.

The Vulgate

The "sweetest fruit of the arduous cultiva-
tion"[40] of Jerome's study of Greek and Hebrew
was his translation of the Old Testament into
Latin from the original Hebrew. Up to that time,
Christians of the Roman empire could read the
Bible in its entirety only in Greek. The books of
the New Testament had been written in Greek;
a complete Greek version of the Old Testament
also existed, the so-called Septuagint, the translation made by the Jewish community of Alex-
andria around the second century before Christ.
Yet for readers of Latin, there was no complete
version of the Bible in their language; only some
partial and incomplete translations from the
Greek. To Jerome and those who continued his

---

[39] Cf. Apostolic Exhortation *Evangelii Gaudium*,
152.175: *AAS* 105 (2013), 1083-1084.1093.

[40] Cf. *Ep.* 52, 3: CSEL 54, 417.

work belongs the merit of undertaking a revision and a new translation of the whole of Scripture. Having begun the revision of the Gospels and the Psalms in Rome with the encouragement of Pope Damasus, Jerome, from his cell in Bethlehem, then started the translation of all the Old Testament books directly from the Hebrew. This work lasted for many years.

To complete this labour of translation, Jerome put to good use his knowledge of Greek and Hebrew, as well as his solid training in Latin, employing the philological tools he had at his disposal, in particular Origen's *Hexapla*. The final text united continuity in formulas by now in common use with a greater adherence to the Hebrew style, without sacrificing the elegance of the Latin language. The result was a true monument that marked the cultural history of the West, shaping its theological language. Jerome's translation, after initially encountering some rejection, quickly became the common patrimony of both scholars and ordinary believers; hence the name "Vulgate".[41] Medieval Europe learned to read, pray and think from the pages of the Bible translated by Jerome. In this way, "sacred Scripture became a sort of

[41] Cf. Apostolic Exhortation *Verbum Domini*, 72: *AAS* 102 (2010), 746-747.

'immense lexicon' (Paul Claudel) and 'iconographic atlas' (Marc Chagall), from which both Christian culture and art could draw".[42] Literature, art and even popular language have continually been shaped by Jerome's translation of the Bible, leaving us great treasures of beauty and devotion.

It was due to this indisputable fact that the Council of Trent, in its decree *Insuper*, affirmed the "authentic" character of the Vulgate, thus attesting to its use in the Church through the centuries and bearing witness to its value as a tool for the purpose of study, preaching and public disputation.[43] Yet the Council did not seek to minimize the importance of the original languages, as Jerome never stopped insisting, much less forbid undertaking a comprehensive translation in the future. Saint Paul VI, following the indication of the Fathers of the Second Vatican Council, desired that the work of revising the Vulgate be brought to completion and placed at the service of the whole Church. Thus in 1979 Saint John Paul II, in the Apostolic Constitution

[42] SAINT JOHN PAUL II, *Letter to Artists* (4 April 1999), 5: *AAS* 91 (1999), 1159-1160.

[43] Cf. DENZIGER-SCHÖNMETZER, *Enchiridion Symbolorum*, ed. 43, 1506.

Scripturarum Thesaurus,[44] promulgated the typical edition called the "Neo-Vulgate".

Translation as inculturation

By his translation, Jerome succeeded in "inculturating" the Bible in the Latin language and culture. His work became a permanent paradigm for the missionary activity of the Church. In effect, "whenever a community receives the message of salvation, the Holy Spirit enriches its culture with the transforming power of the Gospel".[45] Here a kind of circularity is established: just as Jerome's translation is indebted to the language and culture of classical Latin, whose influence is very evident, so his translation, by its language and its symbolic and highly imaginative content, became in turn an impetus to the creation of a new culture.

Jerome's work of translation teaches us that the values and positive forms of every culture represent an enrichment for the whole Church. The different ways by which the word of God is proclaimed, understood and experienced

----

[44] 25 April 1979: *AAS* 71 (1979), 557-559.

[45] Apostolic Exhortation *Evangelii Gaudium*, 116: *AAS* 105 (2013), 1068.

in each new translation enrich Scripture itself since, according to the well-known expression of Gregory the Great, Scripture grows with the reader,[46] taking on new accents and new resonance throughout the centuries. The entrance of the Bible and the Gospel into different cultures renders the Church ever more clearly "a bride bedecked with jewels" (*Is* 61:10). At the same time it witnesses to the fact that the Bible continually needs to be translated into the linguistic and mental categories of each culture and generation, also in the secularized global culture of our time.[47]

It has been rightly pointed out that an analogy exists between translation as an act of "linguistic" hospitality and other forms of hospitality.[48] This is why translation does not concern language alone but really reflects a broader ethical decision connected with an entire approach to life. Without translation, different linguistic communities would be unable to communicate among themselves; we would close the doors of history to one another and negate the pos-

---

[46] *Homilia in Ezechielem* I, 7: PL 76, 843D.

[47] Cf. Apostolic Exhortation *Evangelii Gaudium*, 116: *AAS* 105 (2013), 1068.

[48] Cf. P. RICOEUR, *Sur la traduction*, Paris, 2004.

sibility of building a culture of encounter.[49] In effect, without translation there can be no such hospitality; indeed hostility would increase. A translator is a bridge builder. How many hasty judgments are made, how many condemnations and conflicts arise from the fact that we do not understand the language of other persons and fail to apply ourselves, with firm hope, to the endless demonstration of love that translation represents.

Jerome too had to counter the dominant thought of his time. If the knowledge of Greek was relatively common at the dawn of the Roman Empire, by his time it was already becoming a rarity. He came to be one of the best experts in Greco-Christian language and literature and he undertook a still more arduous and solitary journey when he undertook the study of Hebrew. If, as it has been said, "the limits of my language are the limits of my world",[50] we can say that we owe to Saint Jerome's knowledge of languages a more universal understanding of Christianity and one steeped more deeply in its sources.

[49] Cf. Apostolic Exhortation *Evangelii Gaudium*, 24: *AAS* 105 (2013), 1029-1030.

[50] L. WITTGENSTEIN, *Tractatus Logico-Philosophicus*, 5.6.

With the celebration of this anniversary of the death of Saint Jerome, our gaze turns to the extraordinary missionary vitality expressed by the fact that the the word of God has been translated into more than three thousand languages. To how many missionaries do we owe the invaluable publication of grammars, dictionaries and other linguistic tools that enable greater communication and become vehicles for "the missionary aspiration of reaching everyone"![51] We need to support this work and invest in it, helping to overcome limits in communication and lost opportunities for encounter. Much remains to be done. It has been said that without translation there can be no understanding:[52] we would understand neither ourselves nor others.

Jerome and the Chair of Peter

Jerome always had a special relationship with the city of Rome: Rome was the spiritual haven to which he constantly returned. In Rome he was trained as a humanist and formed as a Christian; Jerome was a *homo Romanus*. This bond arose in

[51] Apostolic Exhortation *Evangelii Gaudium*, 31: *AAS* 105 (2013), 1033.

[52] Cf. G. STEINER, *After Babel. Aspects of Language and Translation*, New York, 1975.

a very particular way from the Latin language of which he was a master and which he deeply loved, but above all from the Church of Rome and especially the Chair of Peter. The iconographic tradition anachronistically depicts him wearing the robes of a cardinal as a sign of his being a priest of Rome under Pope Damasus. In Rome he began to revise the earlier translation. Even when jealousies and misunderstandings forced him to leave the city, he always remained strongly linked to the Chair of Peter.

For Jerome, the Church of Rome is the fertile ground where the seed of Christ bears abundant fruit.[53] At a turbulent time in which the seamless garment of the Church was often torn by divisions among Christians, Jerome looked to the Chair of Peter as a sure reference point. "As I follow no leader save Christ, so I communicate with none but Your Holiness, that is, with the Chair of Peter. For this, I know, is the rock on which the Church is built". At the height of the controversy with the Arians, he wrote to Damasus: "He that does not gather with you scatters; he that is not of Christ is of antichrist".[54] Consequently Jerome could also

[53] Cf. *Ep.* 15, 1: CSEL 54, 63.
[54] Ibid., 15, 2: CSEL 54, 62-64.

state: "He who is united to the Chair of Peter is one with me".[55]

Jerome was often involved in bitter disputes for the cause of the faith. His love for the truth and his ardent defence of Christ perhaps led him to an excess of verbal violence in his letters and writings. Yet he lived for peace: "I wish for peace as much as others; and not only do I wish for it, I ask for it. But the peace which I want is the peace of Christ; a true peace, a peace without rancour, a peace which does not involve war, a peace which will not reduce opponents but will unite friends".[56]

Today more than ever, our world needs the medicine of mercy and communion. Here I would like to say once again: let us offer a radiant and attractive witness of fraternal communion.[57] "By this all will know that you are my disciples, if you have love for one another" (*Jn* 13:35). This is what Jesus, with intense prayer, asked of the Father: "that they may all be one… in us… so that the world may believe" (*Jn* 17:21).

---

[55] Ibid., 16, 2: CSEL 54, 69.

[56] Ibid., 82, 2: CSEL 55, 109.

[57] Cf. Apostolic Exhortation *Evangelii Gaudium*, 99: *AAS* 105 (2013), 1061.

At the conclusion of this Letter, I wish to address an appeal to everyone. Among the many tributes paid to Saint Jerome by later generations, one is that he was not simply one of the greatest scholars of the "library" from which Christianity was enriched over the course of time, beginning from the treasury of sacred Scripture. It could also be said of Jerome that, as he himself said of Nepotianus, "by assiduous reading and constant meditation he made his heart a library of Christ".[58] Jerome spared no effort in expanding his own library, which he always viewed as an indispensable workshop for understanding the faith and the spiritual life; in this way he serves as a fine example also for the present time. But he did not stop there. For him, study was not limited to the years of his youthful training, but a continual commitment, a daily priority. We can say that he became himself a library and a source of knowledge for countless others. Postumianus, who traveled throughout the East in the fourth century in order to explore the growth of monasticism and spent some months with Jerome, saw this

[58] *Ep.* 60, 10; CSEL 54, 561.

with his own eyes. As he wrote: "[Jerome] is always occupied in reading, always at his books: he takes no rest day or night; he is perpetually either reading or writing something".[59]

In this regard, I often think of the experience a young person can have today entering a bookshop in his or her city, or visiting an Internet site, to look for the section on religious books. In most cases, this section, when it exists, is not only marginal but poorly stocked with works of substance. Looking at those bookshelves or webpages, it is difficult for a young person to understand how the quest of religious truth can be a passionate adventure that unites heart and mind; how the thirst for God has inflamed great minds throughout the centuries up to the present time; how growth in the spiritual life has influenced theologians and philosophers, artists and poets, historians and scientists. One of the problems we face today, not only in religion, is illiteracy: the hermeneutic skills that make us credible interpreters and translators of our own cultural tradition are in short supply. I would like to pose a challenge to young people in particular: begin exploring your heritage. Christian-

[59] SULPICIUS SEVERUS, *Dialogus* I, 9, 5: SCh 510, 136-138.

49

ity makes you heirs of an unsurpassed cultural patrimony of which you must take ownership. Be passionate about this history which is yours. Dare to fix your gaze on the young Jerome who, like the merchant in Jesus' parable, sold all that he had in order to buy the "pearl of great price" (*Mt* 13:46).

Jerome can truly be called the "library of Christ", a perennial library that, sixteen centuries later, continues to teach us the meaning of Christ's love, a love that is inseparable from an encounter with his word. This is why the present anniversary can be seen as a summons to love what Jerome loved, to rediscover his writings and to let ourselves be touched by his robust spirituality, which can be described in essence as a restless and impassioned desire for a greater knowledge of the God who chose to reveal himself. How can we not heed, in our day, the advice that Jerome unceasingly gave to his contemporaries: "Read the divine Scriptures constantly; never let the sacred volume fall from your hand"? [60]

A radiant example of this is the Virgin Mary, evoked by Jerome above all as Virgin and Mother, but also as a model of prayerful reading of

[60] *Ep.* 52, 7: CSEL 54, 426.

the Scriptures. Mary pondered these things in her heart (cf. *Lk* 2:19.51) "because she was a holy woman, had read the sacred Scriptures, knew the prophets, and recalled that the angel Gabriel had said to her the same things that the prophets had foretold… She looked at her new-born child, her only son, lying in the manger and crying. What she saw was, in fact, the Son of God; she compared what she saw with all that she had read and heard".[61] Let us, then, entrust ourselves to Our Lady who, more than anyone, can teach us how to read, meditate, contemplate and pray to God, who tirelessly makes himself present in our lives.

Given in Rome, at the Basilica of Saint John Lateran, on 30 September, the Memorial of Saint Jerome, in the year 2020, the eighth of my Pontificate.

Franciscus

---

[61] *Homilia de Nativitate Domini* IV: PL Suppl. 2, 191.

INDEX

FRANCIS

Apostolic Letter

Scripturae Sacrae Affectus

on the Sixteen Hundredth Anniversary
of the Death of Saint Jerome